THE ALP AT THE END OF MY STREET

THE ALP AT THE END OF MY STREET

Poems by Gary Leising

BRICK ROAD

POETRY PRESS

Cover photo credit: *Breathe: The Emergent Colony* © Carrie Scanga

Library of Congress Control Number: 9780989872416
ISBN-13: 978-0-9898724-1-6

Published by Brick Road Poetry Press
P. O. Box 751
Columbus, GA 31902-0751
www.brickroadpoetrypress.com

Brick Road logo by Dwight New

For Melinda, Jude, and Ewan,
who joyfully scale
the neighborhood Alp
with me every day

Acknowledgments

Thanks to the editors of the following publications for accepting individual poems from this collection, sometimes in different forms:

After Ever After: "Fastened to a Dying Animal"
Birmingham Poetry Review: "Heaven as Las Vegas"
Blackbird: "Afterlife"
Buzzard Picnic: "Igg"
The Cincinnati Review: "The Sugar Mouse"
The Connecticut Review: "Ash Wednesday" and "Elvis Presley's
        Recurring Dream, Which I Have Been Having Since His
        Death"
Connotation Press: "Windows" and "You'll Never Walk Alone"
The Cortland Review: "On the Dictionary's Marginal Illustrations"
Crab Orchard Review: "Lincoln's Doctor's Dog"
CutBank: "What the Doctor Said"
Indiana Review: "Thankful" and "Toenails Diary"
Litchfield Review: "Apteka" and "Birdsong"
Margie: "A Pedestrian Poem"
Paterson Literary Review: "Two Crucifixes Hang in My Church"
poem, home: an anthology of ars poetica: "The Poem as Airplane
        Passenger"
Poemeleon: "Worse News"
Prairie Schooner: "Begging at a Statue"
River Styx: "Aliens Abduct Man Nightly" and "Scientists Say Deep
        Space Gamma Ray Bursts Come from Alien Nuclear Wars"
Sewanee Theological Review: "Neither My Wife Nor I Will Clean the
        Bathroom"
South Carolina Review: "Robert Lowell on Damariscotta Lake" and
        "Killer Whale Swallows Marine Park Tourist"
Sou'wester: "Pro-life" and "Walking to Church on Shiloh Street,
        Early Sunday Morning"

Squaw Valley Review: "After Being Asked, While Cleaning Up From A Dinner Party, Why I Do Not Keep A Compost Pile"

Visiting Dr. Williams: Poems Inspired by the Life and Work of William Carlos Williams: "William Carlos Williams at Paterson Falls"

VQR Instapoetry: "Divorce Ceremony"

Whiskey Island Magazine: "The Living Nativity Takes a Break"

The Writer's Almanac: "Your Punishment in Hell"

Several of the poems in this collection have appeared in the chapbook *Fastened to a Dying Animal,* (Pudding House Publications, 2010), and a few others in the chapbook *Temple of Bones* (Finishing Line Press, 2013).

Grateful thanks, too, to Utica College's Office of Academic Affairs, Faculty Resource Committee, and School of Arts and Sciences for various grants to support the writing and revision of these poems.

CONTENTS

ONE

Afterlife 3

Thankful 4

My First Word 5

Pro-life 6

The Living Nativity Takes a Break 7

The Sugar Mouse 8

Occurrence 9

Walking to Church on Shiloh Street, Early Sunday Morning 10

Later That Night 11

Diogenes in the Petrified Forest 12

Robert Lowell on Damariscotta Lake 13

Divorce Ceremony 14

William Carlos Willams at Paterson Falls 15

On the Dictionary's Marginal Illustrations 18

Worse News 20

Stolen Vision 22

TWO

Your Punishment in Hell 27

Birthday Invective 29

Revelation 31

Ash Wednesday 32

Two Crucifixes Hang in My Church 33

Before Saint Patrick 34

You'll Never Walk Alone 35

Diogenes in Hell 37

Life of Stone 38

Apteka 39

Igg 43

Fastened to a Dying Animal..................................44

Aliens Abduct Man Nightly....................................46

Heaven as Las Vegas 48

Elvis Presley's Recurring Dream Which I Have Been Having Since
    His Death..49

What the Doctor Said..52

THREE

The World Is Too Much With Us............................55

The Poem as Airplane Passenger...........................57

Dining with Angels 59

Killer Whale Swallows Marine Park Tourist 64

Scientists Say Deep Space Gamma Ray Bursts Come from Alien
    Nuclear Wars...65

Invitation to Dinner..67

Birdsong..69

The Dog Is Digging In the Snow 71

After Being Asked, While Cleaning Up From A Dinner Party, Why
    I Do Not Keep A Compost Pile..........................72

A Pedestrian Poem..79

Windows 81

Neither My Wife Nor I Will Clean the Bathroom 83

My Wife's Brassieres 84

Toenails Diary...85

Begging at a Statue, ...87

Last Words 91

ONE

Afterlife

When you're dirty, it will rain,
the water any temperature you like.
At first light, the rooster tells the truth:
his calling advises the sun.

In your small home
(once home to the three bears)
you'll find a family of foxes.
They'll forage the woods for food,
and drop what they find in your picnic basket.

You'll spend days lying in flowerbeds,
only your face poking through the pansies' thick blanket.
You wait for butterflies to land on your tongue.
Their flavors, matched to wing-colors,
delight you so. Until one day
you swallow a solid black one.
Its taste—licorice and blood—
makes you realize, finally, you're alone.

Thankful

I'm thankful that my mother is my mother
and my mother wasn't Mary Toft, Englishwoman,
who in 1726 gave birth to seventeen rabbits.
I would hate being one of eighteen children,
the only human one, dragging a dustpan around,
sweeping up droppings from every corner of the house,
dropping out of school for a coal mine job
to keep the siblings in lettuce. And, Lord,
in years there's three or four of them—
the neglected ones—who take to incest,
squirt out litter after litter, while Mary,
Mother Mary, has the King's personal physician
shoving a speculum in her, checking
her womb in London. She left me down south,
big brother wiping coal dust from my face,
awake all night chasing off the wolves.
Once I fell asleep and two became canine-snacks
and a neighbor cooked a third in ale.
It's a terrible life, but it's not mine,
thanks to my mother not being Mary Toft.
Though if she had been, at least I'd be British,
maybe studying at Oxford or Cambridge,
where a school maid brings me shaving water,
makes my bed, and presses my cotton shirt
every morning.

My First Word

Written in a book, my mother
kept it with a lock of hair
and inky footprint. The whorls
and curves of that small mark
are like caves now,
their swirls a journey to some past,
an unknown earth,
some mazy haze where, far off,
water drips into a pool.
Pale algae fuzzes its surface.

The lock of hair is tied with yarn
faded to whiteness, its starting color
now absent as the letters of my word
(my mother wrote in pencil),
my length and weight at birth,
or the date of my first tooth:
all faded in time, erased—
that tooth pushed out by others,
my measurements grown to today's size,
my first word replaced by these,
what I put down here, more words
waiting to vanish, replaced
by the word I say next,
each word leading to one exhaled,
desperate from my deathbed.

Pro-life

Because my freshman-year roommate had no values,
because he stole my money, because he slept
with a different girl each weekend, because I hated
my young scholar's life held against his *carpe diem*
drunk on Thursday-afternoon freedom, because I was
pro-life, I took the condoms he kept in a bowl
and drew the thinnest sewing needle I could find
through the center of each semi-rigid package. A tiny smell,
the whiff of antiseptic wipe torn open before a nurse
gives you a shot, hung over the bowl as I refilled it,
I thought of the tiny void, an army charging for it,
the British at Harfleur, diving man-by-man through
a hole of jagged stones: Gloucester and Clarence;
King Harry with a sword held high; red-faced Bardolph,
yet to be hanged; Pistol carrying a rusty, infectious dagger;
and the boys behind, one-by-one, baggage on their backs,
naïve boys bearing all of this world they'll ever know.

The Living Nativity Takes a Break

Someone comes to feed and water the cows.
Joseph and the shepherds head out back
to split a pack of Camels.

Mary hides her chewed-away fingernails in her sleeves
and thinks about her bills.
Neither young nor pure,

she hands the baby to its mother to feed.
The woman puts her nipple in the baby's mouth,
and doesn't think that this infant

is not a king,
will not perform miracles,
will never feel iron nails in her wrists or ankles,

and will never leave an imprint of her face
on the handkerchief of a merciful woman
who steps out of the crowd.

The Sugar Mouse

The bag, a pound of sugar, all gone
to a mouse, a pest who turned it
to droppings speckling the shelf.
"If it jumps out, I'll scream," she said.
A tiny room to her, the pantry made a world
of places for a mouse to hide.
It could be behind those cans, in that box.
She set out traps. They went unsprung.
Her oldest son, the one who trapped mice
or killed the yard's black snakes,
was a month into his tour,
and she could only say, "He's there,
that country," pointing at the globe.
Cities small as the specks of mouse shit
she thought might make her sick
dotted Iraq's small, tan mass.
The mouse was a machine, divinely planned,
its bowels worked neat as a theorem,
sugar and something equals something else.
She started scrubbing shelves.
She figured equations, the factors in her life:
the creator of the mouse made her.
And she cleaned and cleaned,
then would buy more sugar.

Occurrence

Springtime crows swarm my neighbor's yard,
pile themselves in one spot near the barrel
his old dog lives in. My wife and I wondered
all winter how much longer the limping mutt
would last. *We have our answer*, I say,
as two crows break from the pile, pull
between them something string-like, long, fleshy,
and dripping blood. That dog was nothing
but mean, and wouldn't you be, tied up
to a barrel, left outside all year, fed scraps.
I feel bad for the dog's life, not its death,
she says as the old man runs outside,
waving a rake, swatting crows and crying,
Go to hell. Hell. The dog steps from its barrel,
bloody-mouthed. The last crow leaves.
The old man kneels by the fleshy pile,
picks up a child's scarlet hat.

Walking to Church on Shiloh Street, Early Sunday Morning

Between two parked cars, a dead possum,
on its back, with babies scrabbling at its belly,
some pressing forepaws against teats, squeezing
for what milk there might be.

You walked on, I squeezed one unguarded nipple:
milk spurted. Two lapped drops
from the cold skin, another sucked the nipple
and my finger. A dog would probably get them

by nightfall. I squeezed again, the nipple
a little pink Alp, sucked to a point
by these, old enough to have open eyes,
hair, the exact arrow look of a possum,

but—one clung to my withdrawing hand—
thankfully not the teeth. This mother's body
was a dying earth of its own. Its hairless tail
a wisp of atmosphere, penumbra,

corona, whatever stays visible
as a planet falls in on itself, decaying,
swallowing its falling, smaller moons,
their tails faint streaks of light in some skies.

Later That Night

The earth is not love,
the world houses animals that love,
creatures nesting in hills or valleys.
Your shoulder and hip frame the vale
where my arm settles.
My damp chest presses into your back.

A spur of light falls across the bed
from the broken blind's slat.
Our building's security light glows:
something outside moves,
an animal or tenant coming home.
Almost asleep, the two of us
are a pool on the bed. We each breathe
like slow water's flow,
settle, then pulse.

Diogenes in the Petrified Forest

His empty cup and bowl rattle in his hands
as he walks from tree to tree, from the stalk
remains of a fern to the fallen, broken log
large enough to sit on and think. No begging
calls forth the palest green leaf-bud. No
cajoling summons new sprouting limbs.

Here he is happiest. He would give cup
after cupful of water to keep these stones
alive if he had to. Instead he kneels,
grateful to the universe that made such a place
where plants hold the warmth of day
then the coolness of night in an endless

cycle of something that must be like a love
people cannot feel for each other.
Men and women are warm together and love
that feeling; they are cold apart and hate that.
Here Diogenes only weeps upon seeing traces
left by leaves in a cracked, worn sandstone.

Robert Lowell on Damariscotta Lake

He lifted the sack, and felt the weight
resist him the way the water would
resist his oars when he rowed out straight
from the shore to put an end, for good,
to the whole affair. The heavy weight
of water, stone, and everything else pulled away
from him as he pulled at it.
Behind him, the house shrank closed; he couldn't stay
like the kittens, in a place where he didn't fit.

He put the oars down, drifted, lit a cigarette,
thought of adventures in Boston, forced a smile,
then, a bit Augustinian, thought he'd confess—in a while.
But now, he felt no guilt.
He knocked ash in the water, then he put
the still-lit cigarette in his shirt pocket.
He thought of youth, sadness,
and then it began to burn through;
he suffocated the heat between his palm and chest,
then got on with what he was there to do.

He hoisted the sack, struggled to lift it
while seated. Slowly, to make no splash,
he lowered it into the water, saw the sun flash
off his watch, studied the way light refracted
through water to make his forearms broken.
Then he let go, feeling the canvas slide in
and along his fingers, wet through his palms.

Divorce Ceremony

The reception springs from a science fiction show
she saw where time ran backwards. Family and friends
raise empty crystal flutes to their lips, fill them
with champagne, sip by sip. The straw-colored drink
bubbles up; up it pours into bottles, corked with a pop.

Cellared, riddled, the champagne ages. Opened,
the bottles release the joy of life into a thousand grapes.

William Carlos Willams at Paterson Falls

There, your river,
             the sick river,
                          the falls,
and a couch going
             over
                          but first hanging
up in the outcropping tree,
             upward thrusting
                          among the rapids.

It seems you conjured
             the whole scene,
                          held the couch there
long enough
             to study its floral pattern
                          like wallpaper

then you pushed it over
             without thought of the iron-
                          clang concrete of consequence,
its abstract whirl
             and definition followed
                          by the bottle you sucked
until age six,
             the lock-out in a snowstorm
                          on Passaic St.,
the dollar Pop paid
             you to read Darwin,
                          Darwin himself goes over
the falls—
             gray-bearded photograph

                    glue-stuck to the hardback cover.

Seedy but not slummy,
          every Erie RR station
                   smells and sounds the same
to you;
         toss them all over.
                  Someone at the bottom
sorts them out,
         sorts Pound in London
                 from the Hyde Park sheep
as they splash,
         the Elgin marbles irrelevant
             thudding into a breakwater ring.

Your English-Spanish-French-
         Jewish blood spits
                 its own tributary falls-ward,
your American attitude
         a moment of theft,
                 the slattern of a new mother
in soiled dressing gown
         as you examine her
              on house call rounds,

her child, say all's well,
         and you will take
                 one of the pink curlers
from her dirty brown hair.
         It goes over the falls,
              beneath the whirl and rush,
eddying unseen
         beneath modern poetry,
             its books, their

explication de texte

        all gone to you, you there

              at river's edge,

thinking of that mother

       and the other patients

            you lusted after,

thinking of the woman

       who called that morning

            as you wrote a poem.

You said, "Your child

       swallowed a mouse?

            Get her to swallow

a cat!"

       You hung up the phone

           so hard its bell

rang and rang

       in your ears,

            still rings around you,

you, who in years

       hears Flossie

           read Marjorie Kinnan Rawlings

to you, blind.

On the Dictionary's Marginal Illustrations

Pliers balance above *The Thinker*'s head.
He's not there for art's sake, but to demonstrate—
and contemplate—the meaning of *plinth*, the block
or slab on which a statue rests. Below the *plinth*
rests a *plow*, not a wooden one slowly cutting
earth behind a horse, but a metal, tractor-borne
industrial beast with an array of blades:
they shine like wicked teeth.

Plowboy and *plowman* are defined, not shown.
Plow steel is high strength, used not in plows
but wire ropes. *Plowshare* is a simple noun,
its picture a basic sketch, a blade
made in eight quick lines, and nowhere described
as beaten from a *sword*, whose entry shows
an ornamental saber, the hilt all jeweled
(while the hilt for *hilt* is functional, a cage to guard
the hand), the blade engraved:
art's beauty helps define this tool of war.

But art emerges for its own sake—the whaler
in *scrimshaw* or a detail from Cezanne's
The Pond illuminating *post-impressionism*.
Art also shows us fantasy:
a Grecian urn depicts a *satyr*; pages later
I find *The Hermes of Praxiteles*. He leans,
one-armed, against a tree trunk, on which the crying baby,
Dionysos, sits. To quiet him, Hermes
flashes an Olympian diamond. The child reaches for the
          stone
lost with the missing arm.

(What gifts the gods keep from us!) But here
his only purpose is to show a *strut*,
the marble brace between the tree trunk and his hip.

So much is here to show us something else.
One picture confused me as a child, when I heard
my aunt was sick. I looked up *cancer*, found
the constellation next to the disease's definition.
The stars were her cells, dots of every size,
black points clustering in strange shapes.
Although solid lines connected those dots,
I had to stretch my mind to see the crab.

Worse News

Landing last night in Hawaii, the duck checked messages:
His doctor—*Call me, I have bad news.*
He drank rum punch all morning before remembering.

—*What's up*—*I have bad news. And worse news now.*—*Tell me.*
—*The bad news is you have one day to live. The worse,*
I couldn't get a hold of you yesterday to say so.

So there's this duck. He'll die today watching
a crowded beach of kids and surfers and tanning people.
His white feathers flush red. You ask,

why a duck? I say, because you might not laugh
if he was a man who'd saved up for this trip,
blew his savings on airfare, used his vacation days

to head to the Pacific where he'd die. And what
about the helicopter tour tomorrow he'd prepaid?
Does that future matter? The past? The present?

Why didn't he go visit Mom, the way he always does
on his week off. And what about the cliché office girl
he secretly loves but never asked to go

to see a play, an art show, or eat a five-course meal?
Both she and he are shy, bookish, awkward,
and have been single so long that this trip, today,

changes so little in the world. That man, what would he do?
He'd seize the day and take a surfing lesson—why not?
The sea's right there, and he could spend his last day

paddling out, then trying to balance all the way back to
        shore,
one endlessly repeated act he'd fail at, falling again
and again until nothing was left for him to do.

But cheer up, it's a duck, no man. The duck waddles
        unseen
into the sea and goes, paddling out. His body seems still
though his feet kick like mad, until he stops, alone,

a small white dot lost, floating on the salty, tossing sea.

Stolen Vision

"I cannot rub the strangeness from my sight"

I did it first at a Chinese restaurant:
a resting pair of glasses magnified a menu
on a nearby table. The lenses enlarged one word:
TAKE. I did. The night rained. My wiper blades
only smeared the world. Or those glasses blurred it,
turning headlights into the phlegm
of a dragon's cough or the sprays
from its paired, irritated nostrils.

The second time, at the pool,
theft-brave, I climbed the lifeguard's chair.
The woman asked if I'd seen her eyeglasses.
(Viewed through them and through
a chlorine haze, she'd lost twenty pounds.)
I asked her out; she said okay.
People don't notice their frames
on someone else. Before our date,
I'd swiped a pair of Italian shades.

She wore black. I lost interest in her,
and she faded into the night—
or it bled through her. She waited
at the bar for our table while I went
to the restroom. Someone whose order
took too long was puking tequila sunrises
into the sink. He'd rested
his glasses on the soap dispenser.
They disguised me out the door.

I watched bad days disappear
into night. Then a woman might hover
above the next barstool
and ask about my sign. Rare
were the times I took off glasses
when bedroom lights were still on.
If we watched TV, I wore them.
They made the actors' faces nova
then shrink to the twinkling of far-off stars.

Once a smile asked for my number.
I gave her one from the *If found,*
please notify label of the case and glasses
from the gym locker left open next to mine.
I admit the thefts were wrong, but I needed
each pair and its new way of seeing.
For their owners, lenses are corrective,
but for me, they're speculative.
Bifocals give me options, a monocle

skews depth, thick lenses put everything in fine print.
I got ready for a bigger heist:
contacts—a pair in every tint.
Worn under glasses, I'd have
the vision of two other men.
Four months in, I had ninety pair
and a constant need for aspirin.
My eyes felt swollen as large
as a hay-fevered dragon's.

Analgesics and antihistamines
ate away my stomach lining.
To look into me, a doctor knocked me out:
a camera formed the eye

at the end of a tube he snaked down my throat.
I took one of his endoscopes
to see into other people,
but I couldn't tell an ulcer from a polyp
or a liar from a saint.

My eyes were failing,
my sight was false and every patch
of air was thick as green art deco glass.
Night and day traded places;
sleeping through the light became
my only painkiller. I drove
by feel: the right front tire
bounced off the curb or sparks sprayed
a glow along a row of cars parallel parked.

When my driver's license expired, I failed
the eye test—
every letter was a filled in O.
The last of my vision was gone,
I thought, as I drove home,
slow, gauging speed against the red
of stop signs, traffic signals, brake lights,
swirling sirens, symbol of martyrdom
and sacrifice, the glow that broke my black sight.

TWO

Your Punishment in Hell

Someone will douse a cobra in gasoline,
light the sucker, and shove it headfirst
down your throat. It'll speed straight
through your esophagus, unfurl
its hood to fill your stomach
then begin to strike and strike and strike
and strike and strike: fangs pierce
your stomach, venom pours in,
the little burn of incipient ulcers
grows quick, paralysis sets in.
Your lungs stop before your brain,
before your hand, which lifts
to your mouth the plastic-lidded
paper cup holding the carmel
macchiato cappuccino with a double
shot of espresso and frothed soy milk
topped with two shakes of cinnamon
and no (NO, yes you said *no* twice)
sugar that was made for you
slowly, while I, already running late,
waited behind you for simple,
already-made black coffee.
You will lose all motion before
that drink reaches your mouth,
but you recover and the drink,
strangely, has vanished, and barrista
and cobra-douser-slash-lighter do it all again
and again. I know this because,
for my angry impatience,
I am behind you in line in hell

forever, the pot of black coffee
behind the counter steaming,
turning, I know, bitter.

Birthday Invective

May your baker frost your chocolate cake with mud.
May he mistake, for said mud, the contents of a week's
        worth
of his son's diapers. May the spot just appearing on your
        toe
be not cancer, as you fear, but a fungus-fuzz coating your
        skin.
May the candles on your cake be made from fat
sucked out during your last liposuction,
and when you realize—*the horror!*—that fat is melting
into the creamy chocolate, may you be unable
to change expression because of botox
(may excess botulinum toxin rot your eyes).
May your cat explode in its litter box,
spreading its entrails like those of Jack the Ripper's
last victim, the one he had the most time with,
surgically de-organed. But—good news—
you haruspicate with Tigger's intestines
(may they still leak wet, undigested cat food
as you do!) and discover that handsome doctor
will go out with you. Afterward, may he,
thinking he's emailing the friend who set you up,
email you to say, "That woman's face
reminds me of the slides of spirochetes
from the urethras of 18th century French prostitutes
we studied in med school virology."
May the bread you break alone at dinner after reading that
be studded with shards of safety glass,
and may the wine toasting your birthday
be laced with about-to-hatch spider eggs.
May the medicine you take to kill

the spiders cause you to grow hair everywhere,
everywhere like a German wood-carved statue
of Mary Magdalene. As you live alone
in head to toe wraps and black pashminas,
may your reputation be a Biblical outcast's—
a leper's, a cripple's, an about-to-be-stoned-divorcee's—
may you await a kind, forgiving Son of God.

Revelation

When the sky chokes on dust, when the earth
glows with heat, even the stones cry out.
When winter rises through deserts and spring
brings man to his knees as he watches
some fading beasts fall, then the stones cry out.

When two people go to bed, wake, leave for work,
one returns, says the other's name to no one,
to the carpet, the lamp, the slowly dying houseplant
that's given up on reaching for the sun,
all names begin to vanish, the stones cry out.

When a woman leans against a mantle, touches a mirror
with her fingers, parts from her reflection, flows back into
         it,
rain sprays rivulets over rocks,
erodes into streams, cuts time into the earth,
and the scar on her chin is darker in the mirror, stones cry
         out.

When children are lost, the worst fairy tales come true,
when storytellers speak in tongues, lead the children
through a hole in the ground to the next world
where all stones shatter to sand, when stories fail,
the stones cry out, they cry out, they cry out.

Ash Wednesday

The priest tells his story again:
in his youth, his holistic healing days,
he gave massages to cancer patients.
As their tumors grew, their muscles
shrank. The tissue between skin
and bone—like colored paper filling
an empty gift bag, hiding other paper—
felt like ashes in his young hands.

He'd pull it from the bone,
let it fall like dust. It was nothing
like the back or legs
of the woman he then loved,
her body like clay, not hardened
but not pliable enough to hold the shapes
his fingers made.
                    In months,
her muscles were like ash,
then her body was ash,
sprinkled, windblown, on the beach.

Two Crucifixes Hang in My Church

The hard-to-see features on the gold one
don't convince that this Christ suffers.
The wooden cross in back hangs so high above the door,
you have to know it's there so you don't miss it.
Its face shows no pain, no expression.
Painted blood drips around the crown, at the hands and
        feet,
and in a streak from the enrobed side.
The straight mouth, staring eyes, and unwrinkled brow
show this Christ has cried out in Hebrew to His God.

On TV I saw a Filipino man who,
as his wife neared death during childbirth,
promised God he'd be crucified if the mother and baby
        lived.
They did. On Good Friday he was one of many men
who wore barbed wire crowns and carried crosses through a
        crowd.
Straps bound his wrists tight to the wood
and he placed his feet on a small platform.
Before the cross was raised, two men drove nails through
        his palms.
The nails were thin and had large heads—
like oversized thumbtacks. He bled.
The cross was vertical for minutes, and he screamed.
The two men brought him down, pulled out the nails.
Quickly the blood clotted into pinprick wounds.
He then walked seven miles home, where his wife and child,
unable to imagine a world without his faith, waited.

Before Saint Patrick

Imagine a man of faith sailing, by mistake,
to Irish shores. Imagine that man hungry,
thirsty and looking for a spring, a river.
Salmon leap, splash their way upstream,
and that man, a Christian, walks inland,
drinking from the salmon river, wishing
he could hook a fish and eat the whole,
beastly thing. Eventually he finds a man,
quite mad, who offers food. They struggle
to communicate. The man of faith
speaks perfect French. The madman mutters
Gaelic, and everything sounds like a curse
to the Frenchman and his faith. He wants
to travel back to Brittany, buy a mule
and ride to Rouen. There he will buy
fine clothes, well-cooked rabbit, delicate
vegetables, and he will pray thanksgiving
in the cathedral's polished pews. But
the madman has built a fire, over it
cooks not the metallic red meat they shared
for days, but a salmon, whole, larger
than the Frenchman had seen since landing.
They eat the opaque flesh as evening
settles down its mist. Never before
have the hills looked so huge, so green.

You'll Never Walk Alone

The road to Emmaus, a third man
joins two others. They talk about strange things
happening in the city behind. They do not
burst into song the way men in musicals do.

In *Carousel*, after a suicide, one woman
sings to comfort another. *You'll never
walk alone*, she croons. No one, in my life,
sings to me. My wife sings with the radio,

but the meaning doesn't add up:
I can't get no satisfaction, she sang
on her last birthday, before
I gave her gifts. Those two men met

a third outside Emmaus. No songs
but they still dined with him. Years later
T.S. Eliot thought of them when reading
a polar explorer's journal. He swore

he saw another man plodding in the snow—
a mere phantom. Did that vanishing man
sing an icy song or hum Beethoven
in hope some crashing note might crack

the coldness in the sky? Songs persist:
that suicide is gone, but the words
sung to his wife echo at football games.
In Liverpool the fans serenade their team—

You'll never walk alone—before each game.
The goal's sad nets hang in the breeze.
What words might Christ have sung
after breaking bread, taking wine,

and giving his blessing to those two in Emmaus?
He chewed, swallowed, his mouth was clear,
He smiled. Those two recognized him,
awaited their Lord's words. He disappeared.

Diogenes in Hell

For not believing, seal him in a box, vault
        the box in a wall with no marker.
His soul will turn and turn in joy at touching
        only the box's bare, square walls.

For throwing away all that was given to him,
        let him throw away a stone forever,
let it swing back to him, let him throw it again.
        He will take joy in the eternal tossing.

In this world he starved his body; in the next
        let him be brittle, his limbs breaking like
downed branches in autumn. Grateful
        shall he be to need food no longer,

for even in hell he believes he shall have ideas,
        have a mind to birth thoughts. Let him suffer
all those punishments and more yet let him think
        and he shall not believe in hell. Let him

then no longer think but be only aware of body
        and aware of the thoughtlessness of his mind.
Let his hands hold his brain, his eyes look upon it
        to remind him he thinks not. Then he knows hell.

Life of Stone

His body refuses its breath.
A machine pumps and he shivers,
oxygen feeds him through plastic.

In some way, it is right
that he turns to stone from within,
that his lungs become real rock

under the weight of his chest,
compressed to the green
sheen of an emerald

grasped by the ribs.
This is how I want it to end:
the last animal hour,

slow-moving time forming stone,
creature traded for crystal, glowing
like a thing at the center of earth

beneath some watchful eye,
released from the pressure
of a creator's hands.

Apteka

Sick with a sore throat, under the pharmacy's green awning,
I repeat to myself the Russian, *balit gorla, balit gorla.*
Menya balit gorla i, and the phrasebook's *kashal.*
I find a line to a window. The framed pharmacist
looks as friendly as a Russian can to a sick American.
The itch in my throat enters my ears.

I strain to hear the old woman in front of me.
She hands the pharmacist a jar of water.
I understand the word for four. *Cheteri.*
The pharmacist takes out a larger jar, and, with forceps,
plucks four leeches from it, then gently lets them go
into the smaller jar. The opening forceps
remind me of a fisherman releasing a small catfish
both hands coming away at once.
The leeches try to cling to the jar's sides,
slide down, wriggle, and settle on the bottom.

My turn. The black letters on white boxes
are like animal tracks in the snow, slightly familiar,
but, to me, unreadable. I say my phrase—
I have a sore throat. The friendly pharmacist leaves.
I expect leeches. On my neck they'll suck out the infection
turning my throat, the roof of my mouth, my tongue white.

They'll suck out all the language I know,
the few words that help me at Russian restaurants.
They'll drain my English, taking last the words,
throat, leech, and finally the keyhole shape of *I.*
My throat closes, pinches off speech,

pinches off the ends of every word I think to say,
but still, while waiting, I can, strangely, breathe.

Lincoln's Doctor's Dog

The dog lounges everywhere, bored.
His master doesn't do a thing, says few words.
Daylight hours stretch out so long
the dog, the stupid dog, knows something's wrong.
The master mutters about *a mass, a gray mass*
small as this room's corner's points. The dog asks,
whining the way dogs do, for food. It whines, then hides
in this room's corner. The master decides
at odd times to call the maid to let the dog out.
Midnight, the doctor, sleeping, cries out
about the *soft white substance now without*
its noble case, its rigid shell, now mere clay
upon which the nation's hopes perched yesterday.

The maid, a small black lady in gray
scratches the dog's ears each morning. There's little pay
in her work but the pleasure of a friend,
the dog whose shed fur gives her no end
of sweeping work. The doctor waves her in;
she takes away his tray of food, not eaten—
he hasn't eaten a whole meal in days.
She'd tell him but she never stays
in the same room as him. She didn't before
and hasn't since he came in, late, shut the door
and told her the news: *Much has come to its end—*
the only time he spoke as if she were his friend.

The dog curls at his feet while he sleeps
at his desk, hunched over letters in a heap
he means to shovel through the way history
digs ditches through our lives, its mysteries

eroding rivulets into rivers. The dog twitches
as it dreams, yelps gently. The doctor is bewitched
by dreams of the autopsy, the heft
of his patient's organs in his hands as Death,
as an attendant nurse bearing knives,
shows the doctors the futility of human lives.
The doctor wakes and reads the last words he wrote,
the curlicued letters beating on the page, little boats
swirling in a mighty river's eddies,
tiny things sinking, the ink holding them steady.

At night, after the maid goes home,
when the dog gives up on his dry, week-old bone
and paws at a spot in front of the door, waiting
to go out, the doctor gives in, hating
the walk in the District's misty rain, his small
but noble street, stony, curving here like a wheel,
ahead, curving like one wrinkle on the brain
he weighed a week ago. Then he thought, and does again,
now, about the country, the many men he failed
to help in the war's five years, and of one jailed,
and of his patient and friend, the man who lies
entombed. The doctor held his brain, noted its size,
its weight, then took it from the scale's teetering pan:
it weighed as much as the brain of an ordinary man.

Igg

Caveman made that sound and it became
his name. *Igg*, he said to the stick man
drawn on the wall above where he slept,
Igg, he said to the vine he sucked water from,
Igg, he said to the naked woman he met by a fruit tree
who said *Ogg* back. Ogg was the man
she loved who didn't love her, though she
bore his children who both died, and when
they did Ogg beat her, broke her leg
so she walked slow and with a limp, but Igg
only saw her standing and had no idea
her stretch marks were a flaw. She had
dark hair and she said *Ogg* but didn't
really know if that was love but knew Ogg
was where she left him or would return
to that spot where they ate and slept,
so Igg left her without knowing her name.
Igg, he said to the toothy mammal that attacked
later that day, and when he fought it off, *Igg*
he said to the blood in the dust beneath him.

Fastened to a Dying Animal

Someone tied a weasel to my chest,
but it's okay, it's not the flesh-ripping
claws and toothy kind of weasel,
but one that's sick, a brain tumor,
I think. He's so lethargic,
his eyes don't focus on me,
not even when I say his name.
Lisa, I say (I named him when I thought,
erroneously, he was a girl),
and he doesn't look up, or move.
He eats dry dog food soaked in water
to make it soft, and my dog
watches me prepare it. His ears
are perked up, head cocked,
but when I give him none of the mush,
he's not disappointed. But Lisa,
the only time he perks up is when he smells food.
Sometimes he makes a sound.
He'll get better, I think. Other times,
that sound is a cough, and my shirt
gets covered with a yellowish goo
trickling out his mouth. Then I find out
he's not a weasel, but a small,
sick otter, so we get in the bathtub.
He perks up, tries to swim,
but can't move with coordination.
When I sleep, I lie on my back
or side, half-afraid of rolling onto him,
half-thinking that if I did,
I'd end his suffering.
But his downward curving whiskers

look like the unintentional mustache
of an old man who struggles
with the simple task of shaving,
and never cuts away those few,
long hairs.

Aliens Abduct Man Nightly

When I suffer through the loneliness
that feels like no one will ever visit or call,
I count the days since I saw my few friends
and wonder, if I died, how long the corpse
would rot and stink before friends think of me—
it's times like these I hope or fear they'll come
and take me far away in silver spaceships,
take me quickly from a crowded bar. No one
there sees me but the mirror. Its glass perceives
my face from between dusty bottle necks.

The aliens can do what tests they want:
I'll give them samples freely, open wide
for anal probes. Maybe they'll put a chip
beneath my skin and track its silicon
signal, and when I've been alone too long
they'll come to check I'm still alive and safe.

This article describes a man who thinks
these grey, bug-eyed things are holy angels.
If so, why don't they hear my calls for them?
I spend nights on my porch and watch the stars
distorted into twinkles by the screen.
I pick out one and wish it would grow large,
and press through the black fabric of the sky
toward my front lawn's tiny openness
where bats scour the streetlight's glow for food.

They never come. The expectation keeps
my mind from settling on more certain things:
the house, the lawn, the air, the crazy bats

that fly and dive for nothing more than bugs.
There's nothing on earth that wants me here that much,
that jinks and swerves to swallow me alive.

Heaven as Las Vegas

A Friday night landing: you lose your breath
leaving the cloudless sky. Millions of lights
end your tunnel. You had not thought that death
could bring so many to this ageless night.

Nothing's real: the pyramid's polymer façade,
some singer's bad Italian barcarole....
Where, among all this, might one find God?
Your pockets bulge with the part of your soul

you can spare in coins and crisp new bills.
A ball hits red, not black. You're doomed to lose
until three sevens save you. Quarters spill
from slots like grace. An angel brings free booze,

you stumble outside, start the blinding third day
of death. So few seem to have stayed, you think,
as overhead, planes take them all away,
and heaven's Sunday population shrinks.

In one place, many gather around a table
where a croupier wields his stick like a shepherd's rod,
keeping near him a few of the lucky faithful,
those favored, loved by chance, if not by God.

Elvis Presley's Recurring Dream, Which I Have Been Having Since His Death

He's on stage, the young version, belting out an early hit,
　　"Hound Dog" or "That's Alright Mama," or "Shake, Rattle,
and Roll." He's rocking around the microphone stand, more prop-
　　　　slash-dance party partner than support for the mike
he's spraying snarled-out words and saliva at, and he does
his thing so intensely, closes his eyes for each line, opens them,
　　　　notices that, as the song gets one line, one lyric phrase
closer to its inevitable end, large swaths of the crowd—

the teenage boys in white t-shirts and leather jackets, the girls
　　with hair in sprayed-up styles worn just for tonight,
and the chaperoning parents still sitting with *Life* in their laps,
　　　　trying to cover their ears and keep reading the captions
beneath the pictures of Eisenhower and his dog on the White
House lawn—large swaths of that crowd disappear. Poof, vanish
　　　　like the invisible man in the movie but worse, they're
not invisible, but gone, the clothes on their backs,

gone, all gone, and they ain't coming back. It's like
　　Cold War fear made real. The Russians have some weapon
that zaps the youth away, and they focus that
　　　　disintegration ray on rock concerts. Devil music! But no,
　　it's just a dream, and even though Elvis tells guitarist
Scotty Moore, "I'm afraid if the song ends, they'll all be gone,
　　　　but this ain't no record that'll fade out. We could
play forever, man," and Scotty rips into a solo—a long

bluesy dirge predicting what the Grateful Dead'll do in years—
　　and the fans still vanish in sections. Eventually,

Elvis knows (because this is a recurring dream), they'll
        all be gone, even Scotty. Elvis will sit down on stage,
    the spotlight burning its full moon glow where the union worker
who's vanished left it aimed. Looking at that empty glow
            woke up the King of Rock and Roll every night. But now
        since his death, I've had that dream. I'm there, too, way up high

my ticket stamped obstructed view, my seat tucked behind
        a pillar which is stamped *do not climb on*, yet once
the vanishings started, some kid tried to monkey-shimmy
            his way up, like hanging in the rafters would keep him safe
        from whatever the Russians were doing. Elvis still hadn't
been drafted, so he didn't offer any military secrets
            on surviving this catastrophe, just kept on singing "Hound
        Dog" more intensely, like it could save the world

or at least the few thousand people in the concert hall. I'm there
        with my wife and girlfriend. (Yes, with both, because this
is rock and roll, and with Elvis all is possible, all is allowed,
            and because this is a dream, and in it I have both wife
        and girlfriend, and when I wake up and tell my wife, she
can't be mad—though she will—because I can't control
            my dreams; this leads us to a discussion of Freud,
        etc., but isn't the real point not who's with me or what

it means, but that I'm having Elvis Presley's recurring
        dream, and why it's come to me?) Everyone—fans, security,
guitarist, popcorn seller, monkey-boy swinging from rafters—
            has vanished, and then girlfriend goes, which is sad
        for a second, but not really, because she wasn't real and even
if she were, I would know she wouldn't last anyway. That's
            when I look at my wife and know she's going to vanish.
        There are teary-eyes and a moment we both want to say

the big thing but not enough time, not enough time
for our lives together to flash before our eyes and she's gone
and I wasn't even holding her hand, missed out on the feeling
of having my hand filled with hers, squeezing, then empty
suddenly and making a fist. It's just me and Elvis,
me with my obstructed view and him alone, no longer singing.
I lean around the pillar to see what Elvis always knew
would come next, what always woke him up in a sweat:

he ages, alone—young rock idol to G.I. stud to movie star
to Vegas attraction to comeback special jumpsuit hero
practicing kung fu, etc. The scene reminds me of a nature
show with time lapse photography where an injured fox
collapsed, died, its body shrank then bloated up as if it would
explode before it started to decay. There's no one I can tell this to,
I'm alone, and Elvis is a jumpsuit falling inward on itself,
the full moon spotlight hovering behind him.

What the Doctor Said

Imagine a countdown clock, ten, nine
eight, so on, but it's, say, four digits long.

It started at four nines, nine-nine-nine-eight
then down. In a long while, you get to four eights,

the same interval till four sevens. They glow
like hooks on the digital readout. The countdown

clock, you know, by its nature, will stop.
And then: an explosion, or a light somewhere turns on

or off, or the piercing drone of an alarm.
Maybe a rocket launches. Who knows—we know

only the countdown stops. That's your body now,
that's this disease. Here's the thing:

imagine the digits are foreign to you. In time,
you get the sequencing, sort of, know when it will click

to four identical digits, lights arranged all alike.
So when it says six-six-six-seven, the next

could be the last or it could keep going.
No matter what I tell you now

you'll never look away.

THREE

The World Is Too Much With Us

I was everyone on the bus, you said,
there's one Gary, there's another. The third
got off at the last stop, but the fourth
reads the paper, the fifth has one of those devices
you play games on or email with and the sixth
shaves even though the driver (a seventh me)
keeps saying shit about blood-borne pathogens.
But Gary doesn't cut himself—he's that good.
The old woman (whom you name Jane in your telling)
says device-wielding Gary views disgusting pictures.
You weren't sure, but surely saw one with a horse....
Hours later, the teenage girl from the bus tells the cop,
That creepy dude kept looking at me, stalker-like.
I'm sure he followed me home. What did
he look like? *Curly hair, kinda tall,*
slightly off-center nose. Yes, they figure out,
like the cop, exactly. You see a sketch of me
on that night's news. Wanted for creepery.
I'm everywhere in the broadcast. Cab-driving
Gary delivered twins in the backseat during
a snowstorm! Jobless yokel Gary found
a two-headed snake under his porch! Gary
hit a three at the buzzer to win the championship,
and Gary on the losing team will turn pro!
President Gary issues health care reform,
and pundit Gary says, *It's Nazism, pick*
a minority and line them up for the cattle cars
to Birkenau. But who will that be? says first-time-
caller-long-time-viewer Gary. *Women? All us*
men are Catholic blue-eyed German-Americans.
Another Oscar-winning performance from Gary,

this one opposite Angelina, and two channels over,
flip to the funny one, Gary behind a desk mocking
inconsistencies in rhetoric by all those D.C. Garys.
How can they be such fucking morons? asks
your husband Gary, who gets up to take out
the dog. Later he'll grind coffee, pour water,
set the timer for the A.M. and that's the first
Gary-like thing in your narrative, because I
am boring, my friend. I'm a college professor,
it's almost midnight, and twenty of me
sit at a long table, each grading one freshman
comp essay written by some semi-literate kid.
Twenty kids who'd be all right if they wrote like me.

The Poem as Airplane Passenger

At first it's really nothing,
idling in the terminal, too poor
for overpriced bar drinks,
marked-up fast food.

It has explored in every direction,
the numbing repetition of gates,
their waiting crowds growing
from the lines of linked seats.

Soon it will board. But now,
Poem slumps in a vinyl seat,
a foot propped up
on the carryon bag.

First called to board, it takes
an aisle seat. Other passengers
bump its waiting head
with bags as they go by.

A large man squeezes in
the window seat next to it,
spills over the armrest, gains
weight on the tarmac,

his shoulder forces Poem's
torso into the aisle.
The flight attendant's ass
brushes Poem's shoulder

as she checks the security
of every passenger's seat belt,
readies the cabin for takeoff.
Poem is uncomfortable,

but says nothing. Takeoff
awaits. The plane will rise,
air pressures change,
turbulence jar this narrow world.

In this new atmosphere,
Poem will grow, its body
become something new,
filling every empty space.

Dining with Angels

At six your empty house is finally clean.
Your feather duster gathers no gray sign
of dirt's residences. Your many books,
once arranged like a northern sea-town's dikes
across tables, towering around chairs
are organized: art, self-help, home repair,
dirty novels chuffed off to lost ghettoes
(a city's poorest with no place to go).
Books fit like houses on suburban shelves.
Like your mind, its arguing right and left halves,
those shelves portion out all the things you know,
things you forgot, and things you learned to do.
Tonight's that way, too: your wife's with her friends,
you have yours over for a summer's-end
party. Now, chaos destroys spotlessness
in your kitchen. The flour's powdery mess
snows over your counter's long, empty plain.
The factory-like pasta maker strains
and rolls out strips that look like dirty roads.
Soon they'll be filled, then arranged with deft folds;
their gritty spans transformed into pillows,
soft places to rest among the fallen snows.

When the prepping's finished, the water steams
then boils. The angels arrive right on time,
seven of them in white shirts, ties, and slacks,
wings folded flat against their human backs.
There are no putti flitting in corners
like an old painter's framing characters
unfurling legends: *All ready to dine*
or *Gabriel presents the host with wine.*

Well-mannered, they try all the food, though
one or two cut asparagus spears
in pieces, push them from plate's stern to stem
to make it look like some have been eaten.
One breaks the tails off his shrimp with a snap—

the ice they're on must melt like time-lapsed
films in the eyes of these timeless angels.
Its water turns pink, dyed by the shrimp tails,
the beautifully fading translucent tails.

You drink white wine late, and each angel tells
a story. One about a hellish commute,
another how she dispatches the rude
dinnertime "courtesy calls," leaving the phone;
the caller keeps on his pitch, not knowing
his pleas aren't being heard. Another whines
about the warranty on his cell phone,
that didn't cover the waterproof shell.
Are their stories meant to be literal?
Or do they symbolize sinners, sad sky-
tossed prayers, and children doomed to die?

You're tired. They're not, but know it's time to go.
They offer to help clean, you insist, *No,
it's not much work.* One jokes the parsley-greened
cutting board isn't dirty, it's seasoned.
So is the mess the angels leave behind.
Each bottle you opened is full of wine,
leftovers fill all the tupperware you own.
Out your window, you watch the angels turn
the corner, turn into small birds, find nests

in trees nearby. You skip cleaning to rest
and dream of your guests. The trees' dark leaves hide
them from the darker pall of this night's sky.

Penguins Migrating in the Zoo

Leaning as if they want to fall in,
children gather at the exhibit's fence,
excited by these thirty penguins who,
just before Christmas, began circling the pool.

For years, they spent each day at water's edge,
unaware their wild kin would swim from Argentina
to Brazil in search of calmer weather, feeding grounds,
or a place to mate and nest. Now these zoo birds,
streamlined with feathers smoother than skin,
slice through the water. Jockeying for position,

they look like speed skaters, heads down,
bodies bobbing for balance. The space so small,
penguins so many, it's like the Olympic Committee
did away with heats, started all comers at once.

Birds break from the pack when their keeper
dangles a fish near their path. Like an athlete
grabbing water, a runner drinking it in stride,
the penguins don't care
if bits of fish fall from their beaks.
As far as they're concerned, they're dirtying water
that will be miles behind them soon.

What keeps them going? What keeps them from asking,
Didn't we just pass that rock? How will they know
when to stop? All that changes are the people watching.

For once the penguins aren't standing,
statue-like, on the faux-rock-escarpment,

leaning from its ledges, waiting like believers
waited for signs at Medjugorje or Fatima.
No, these penguins have seen the coming of whatever god
or saint reached its glowing hand through the clouds
and pointed their way. When they've made their migration's
final lap, they'll leap from the water,
and rest among these rocks, the world around them new,
every crevice, ledge, and stone waiting to be discovered.

Killer Whale Swallows Marine Park Tourist

We cannot know what made the whale stay down so long
after swallowing the woman who leaned in too far
as if there was something small in the pool she needed to
        see.
Surely the beast was too small to be Biblical,
its blubbered hide too black and white, and the woman
too young and bookish-looking to make a prophet
wombed in the belly, birthed in a plankton-spew
on a far shore. How long could she live in there,
swallowed, it seemed, whole? Could she fight,
maybe rend some gullet membrane, choke the thing
with its own blood? We waited for a sign.

At the bottom of the pool, it spat her body out.
She surfaced, dead, coated with some otherworldly slime.
Her floral dress billowed with the waves, her hair floated
in tangled messes like knotted rags. When we hauled
the corpse ashore, we noticed the delicate glasses—gold
wire-frames—still on her face, unharmed.
One of us removed them to close her staring eyes,
then stuffed them in a pocket, afraid a glance
at their lenses would let us see what she saw
inside the whale, or—even worse—what lies beyond.

Scientists Say Deep Space
Gamma Ray Bursts Come
from Alien Nuclear Wars

Could anyone have lived? Where have they gone?
Maybe they bounced from one world to the next—
a planet, say, of ice, then one of sand,
and, every time they'd just get settled in,
their enemies would find them, having searched
the universe with some tracking device.

The surviving few built up a town, and then
they met the natives, enslaved them on some farms,
or in factories where bigger bombs were built.
Then slaves revolted, and someone out of hand
blew them all to hell or through deep space.

Later, a dark planet became a home
for one stray band. They settled there, raised goats.
By chance they found fuel bubbling beneath
the world's thin, shifting crust. They drilled through it.
Another tribe arrived and killed them for it.
A third took it from them. And so on, until
a fiery bomb ignited those fuel fields.
The world's core burned, its fragile crust collapsed.
It helps to think that someone got away
and hopped from world to world, from rocky cliffs
to vast and lifeless seas.

                              Everywhere
they left a little something—art or tools
or even just a prayer. And then one day
it comes to us. We're carbon, iron, blood,

and all we know of them is gamma rays,
a radiating fire that filled their homes
like ashes filled buildings of Pompeii.

Invitation to Dinner

We'll start the evening with the warmed oven's groan
when my wife opens it and puts the main course in.
The door's noise will startle you; we find it welcoming,
like the tree outside the window.
Its yellowed leaves sag under the early November dusting of
      snow;
some fall. We'll save the label from the wine you'll bring.
The cork can be your souvenir:
let it recall the free-range chicken stuffed with garlic
      cloves—
if you sweat tonight, your sheets will smell of it for days.
Only I know the raw smell of the butchered innards
already removed to the dumpster.
A stray cat or raccoon will feast, trapped after diving
to feed without thought of escape.
It will scare our neighbor throwing out today's newspaper.
With the window open against the oven's heat
we're close enough to hear him shout.
We're close enough to the city's zoo that when traffic is
      light,
we'll hear some animal cry out in fear or for its mate.
I'll guess what beast makes each noise.
"His map of the neighborhood," my wife will say,
"has the acres of the zoo blocked with *here be monsters*."
But there's a crocodile there big as our queen-sized bed,
and once a friend saw a coyote in the park across the street.
But if Cincinnati is TV's *Wild Kingdom*, our home,
dear friend, is a peaceable one for now.
Imagine the exploring Land Rover bouncing
across the savannah, but loaded with food.
Our groaning oven is the fire, the kitchen is camp,

a mess tent rich with basil, cumin,
and wisdom-bestowing sage. Join us, soon.
For tonight, as we sleep in our separate homes,
jackals paw at the doors, baring teeth for scraps.

Birdsong

After he dies, my brother wants to come back as a bird.
Its flight will give a freedom we don't know,
and doing what we want, he said,
is all there is to have on earth. I like the feel
of skin and hair so much that feathers
and the open sky won't call me back to life.

There's a painting by Jack Yeats, a farewell to his brother.
A man—Jack or any Sligo peasant—watches
heavy geese or swans flying out to sea,
their wings set to glide. We know they won't turn back,
these birds of thick-set paint Jack Yeats
once knew as men.

               Why would a man
become a bird? Don't most people want to move *up*
the chain? From bird to beast to man to better man,
you climb to God or some transcendent state
unless somewhere you do wrong.
My neighbor with Down syndrome,
is she paying because the woman she was
last century was poor and let her children starve?
Maybe she's moved up, no longer a gazelle,
the one a leopard singled out. Her throat was crushed;
her herd moved on.

               So who's
to say what's better: my brother's life,
his wife and kids, or some sea bird's unending flight,
its joy diving after fish?
The day my brother's death arrives, his family will hurt,

maybe think time has stopped for them.
What's the chance they'll see migrating birds level to a glide
and think the same thing as Jack Yeats,
who hailed William's arrival from London or France
with a brother's spare kindness,
the way I greet or say goodbye to my own?

The Dog Is Digging In the Snow

I'm freezing at the end of evening's leash, and sure he's dug
a clichéd rut to China or found a natural spa
bubbling to warm his nose. I crouch to dig with him,
alive with hope we'll find some gold or gem-soaked vein
to follow till it comes out summer-warm.
Instead, my bare, cold hand and his hard teeth
meet on the thing he finds: a squirrel, dead;
a piece of bread; or long ago discarded bone.
He'll carry it home proud and bury it right at the door
        before
we go inside to sleep and dream of spring.

What does this mean, me and the dog digging
for different things in the same place? And who
has the better chance of getting what he wants?
I'm not instinct like him, alive to the raw moment of smell.
When this snow melts next month, he'll find that bone
and be surprised. I'll wait till then for all the things
he's planted in our yard to sprout like bulbs:
tulips and daffodils that break the snow's thin crust and die,
reminding me each season's a mere stretch of passing time.

After Being Asked, While Cleaning Up From A Dinner Party, Why I Do Not Keep A Compost Pile

Decay. The one-word answer as I slop
the wet towel over the countertop, its slate,
granite, that will be here even when I'm not.
The cabinet's full of appliances that might
outlast me—their plastic shells at least,
even if motors break down and the blender
or ice cream maker no longer swirls
new foods into being. But that banana,
not here from the store a week, turns black.
The red pepper's seedy core needs only
a few August days to look like some infected
organ plucked from my body and dropped
on an O.R. floor. Less for this avocado half.
Against decay, though, I wouldn't choose
to be the broken blender, no electromagnet
spinning its servos and gears, mere shell still here.
The countertop: let me be the countertop,
lasting. Or let its granite accept a chisel
carving out my name and a pair of dates.

"God Forbid,"

the agent kept saying, "anything should happen to you,"
    and I kept thinking *God won't forbid anything from happening to me*,
    but she had her job, i.e., to sell whole life insurance instead of
        term,
and I have my mortality, and I don't think God will change that,

but, still, she kept imploring God to forbid not only my death,
    but *anything* from happening to me. Then I started hoping
    God would realize the elided word *bad* from her prayer,
because a life where nothing happens sounds pretty dull. God,

though, doesn't really forbid much from happening. Not in the way
    the agent meant. He doesn't step down from heaven, put a
        foot,
    a giant, Sistine-Chapeline-faded-painting-of-a-foot in front
of the Honda about to t-bone into a minivan. Even if there's a
        drunk

at the wheel of that Civic and a single mother with three kids piled
        in the van.
    God lets it go, and doesn't even forbid the irate drunk, who's
        okay
    or drunk enough he doesn't feel the broken leg he's standing
        on,
from hopping out and yelling at the oldest kid, the only one still
        conscious,

because he thinks that kid was driving. If any witness looked up,
    they wouldn't see a Sistine Chapel ceiling sky, but ordinary
        clouds
    assembling above the ordinary wreckage and ordinary blood.

I could be in either one of those cars someday, or rather, I could
  have been,

but now that my agent told God to forbid it… I could only think,
  yeah,
   yeah, I'm going to die, God won't stop that, will he? But let
   him stop
   some certain kinds of death, e.g., being eaten alive by a weasel,
a botched facial peel, or being victim of one of those apocryphal
  stories where

man trips on subway platform as train pulls into station, falls in
  between train
   and platform, his lower half is crushed and ripped apart, but the
   train
   halts, holds him there and stops the blood flow. When the train
moves or the jaws of life cut him free, all his blood drops out, and
  wham,

he's dead. God, please, forbid *that* happening to me not because of
  the pain
   (well, not only because of the pain) but because in those stories
   the man
   gets kept alive long enough to see his wife, and, much as I'd like
   to see
mine one last time before I die, I can't think of what I'd say to her.
  I love you,

yes, of course, but what else and when would I know it's been
  enough, was time
   to say, "Conductor, move this train along," my last line,
   although it sounds
   strangely like the last words of a man on stage about to burst
   into song

in a Broadway show's big dance number, something full of
        trombones and girls

in spangled tights who do high kicks then spin, smiling all the time.
        Another story,
    this one from philosopher Peter Unger: Man sinks his
        retirement
    into a Bugatti, doesn't insure it, parks it on a railroad track's
left branch of a Y. A little kid plays on the right branch. Out of
        control

train hurtles into view, will take the right branch unless Man throws
        the switch,
    but then, bye-bye Bugatti. He doesn't know the kid, but the car
    cost him 1.7 million, plus taxes, license, and registration fees.
        His wife
said that cost more than all the houses they've ever lived in
        combined,

and think of all the travelling they'd do on that money. I don't
        know what
    he said to her, because that bit isn't in Unger's story, but that's
        what
    my wife would say if I wanted a Bugatti. It is what she says
every time I want a supercar, the Nissan GTR, the Pagani Zonda,

the McLaren F1, or the Koenigsegg. And it's her, not Peter Unger's
        man
    I was thinking about, because I realized the agent was talking to
        her,
    not me, with every "God forbid something happen to Gary."
        My wife
is probably thinking that none of the policies we've discussed would
        buy

a Bugatti if I died, but she and the kid could drive the sensibly-
        warrantied
    Hyundai to the airport for all the trips abroad (finally, Australia!)
    for years to come. She knows God won't forbid anything—
        how could he
if he couldn't even forbid what Jesus asked could pass in
        Gethsemane? So I know

the policy's okay, a good investment, sound, because God won't
        forbid actions,
    not in the sense of preventing things from happening, but he
        does
    forbid much if we mean set up interdictions, laws. See
        Leviticus,
full of *thou shalt not*s. "Thou shalt not allow anything to befall the
        purchaser

of whole life, lest I have to pay out on this policy," the agent is
        saying.
    In Gethsemane, Jesus' "sweat was as it were great drops of
        blood
    falling down to the ground," wrote St. Luke, which is my sweat
as everyone discusses my death, which I am now imagining as
        Unger's scene:

on the left end of the Y, the life insurance policy of a Bugatti
        Veyron,
    8 liter engine, 16 cylinders, 1020 brake horsepower, top speed
    253 miles per hour, and the car has 10 radiators, which my wife
        points out,
regularly, is 3.3 times the number of radiators in all the cars I've
        owned in my life,

combined, and it's my life, me, on the Y's right end. I'm reading a
        book,
    or strumming a guitar, or working on my golf game, practicing
        my grip
    on the club and the break of my wrists because it's got to be
        something
small like that bringing that snap hook into play on every damn
        hole.

I'm studying the drawings in Ben Hogan's lesson book so intently I
        don't hear
    the runaway train behind me. I can see my Bugatti over there,
        which
    does not have room for golf clubs except in the passenger seat,
so it's just me out here today, and I have no idea which way the
        switch in the Y

is set, or where it is, but God's not standing by it where he'll decide
        if today's
    the day for a bloody smear on the tracks or a twisted wreck of
        4,486
    pounds of aluminum carbon-fiber and oil. Automobile fluids
or body fluids? Leviticus 15 tells all about bodily fluids: pus,
        semen, menstrual

issue—and isn't that really what we are, the softness of fluid and
        tissue stuck
    onto bones? Jesus was that, too, right? Leviticus offers the
        laws
    on unclean (i.e., menstruating) women, their *issue in blood*. But
        later on,
the blood is referred to as *flowers*. Two roses blooming on the ends
        of a stem's

one Y. Which branch does the train run down today? Right after I
     figure out
     the proper grip, proper swing, proper turn of my hips to face
        the target,
     I start toward my Bugatti, I've got a tee time in 20 minutes, and
        WHAM!
the train speeds over the track I've just stepped from and I think
     only,

That was close, then, *How fast was that thing going?* Probably no more
     than a third
     of the Veyron's top speed as it hurtles me to the country club
     where I think I'll finally have a chance of breaking par, maybe
        playing
in a tournament, earning a few dollars with my game. God forbid
     that ever happen.

A Pedestrian Poem

To the woman at the bus stop
I am the cartoon coyote, frozen,
a foot hangs above the pavement: *Homo Pedestrian*,
the everyday, undistinguished man, bold,
democratic, the way Whitman must have felt
as he wandered through shipyards or passed
escaped slaves on a long dirt road. My steps
could come from *Leaves of Grass*
or Dickinson's poem about hope.

Cars keep coming, ignore the crosswalk sign,
its yellow light, a sun not noticed doing
what it does. *You're keeping this poor man
from work*, my expression says. One car stops,
traffic in the other direction continues, and I
stand on the twin yellow lines, narrow
my waist, following a Pilates instructor's words,
Stand straight as if there's a harness on your head
pulling it to the ceiling as you inhale. I stretch,
afraid of exhaling as side mirrors slip by,
their plastic backs, hip-high, the color of bruises.

The worst cars rush by: the bumper of a Civic
wants to break my legs, an SUV could flatten me,
a Camaro—its chrome-plated dual exhausts shine
like ceremonial daggers—longs for my body
outlined on its hood. Then, some hope,
a block away, a station wagon, its driver
a mother of four grown children. She'll see me,

think of the son she loves the most, the one
who didn't finish college and can't hold
a steady job. She'll stop.

Windows

A heat lamp warms the cold-blooded snakes:
a white-mouthed moccasin, a black-mouthed mamba.
A girl points, says only, *Snake*, over and over.

She follows her saying of this word
through the reptile house, its walls full of caves.
Their windows open on us, my wife and I,
this child, and her parents: teenagers paying
more attention to her than to the animals.

They've gone the same way as us all day:
bears, tigers, insect house. The girl wanders
far enough from her parents, someone entering
might think she's with us. I imagine her
calling me *Dad*, asking if the glass can hold back
the python large enough to kill a child.

But she's secure enough she wants to reach
through the glass to touch each snake,
reach from our world into others:
the sidewinder's Sonoran desert
or what could be our backyard
with a pair of rat snakes.

Each world has its own sun, some food,
the weather's free of hurricane or drought,
skies clear of predatory birds. The green tree snake
twines among many tiny branches, a second
rests in the dirt.

My wife and I watch
our child from a distance. She learns her world,
finds the glass around her. Someone opens
tiny doors in walls painted like sky, dunes,
or ruined rainforest temples. He moves the snakes
with hooks, changes water, prunes a plant.

Someone controls the worlds we watch,
yet we're still scared. We leave this couple with their girl,
happy to leave the snakes, to chance
that in our world no cobra hides in tufts of grass
imported from some place overseas,
some world wholly other than our own.

Neither My Wife Nor I
Will Clean the Bathroom

It's lush and green except where we've worn a tiled path to
        the sink,
the shower, and the commode. My wife tip-toes it—it
        could be,
she says, a game trail; behind the foxtail palm a Komodo
        dragon
might hide, its teeth sharper than the blade on her Gilette.
I tell her not to worry. During her workday, I surveyed
the flora and fauna, am working on a *Field Guide to the
        Bathroom*.
A young dwarf caiman floats in the toilet tank, feeding on
        minnows.
Under the sink, two cobras coil in a home.
Sometimes flashes of snakeskin roll among the toilet paper
        tubes
surrounding the waste can. I've yet to see them feed,
but suspect they stalk the rats and star-nosed moles.
The rodents battle for control of the pipes. We cannot kill
the apex predators—without these reptiles, the small pests
would populate out of control and spill to other rooms:
the rats would nest in our bed and clams bed in the
        dishwasher.
At night we hear the small caiman's helpless cries.
There is no mother to protect it, to carry it in her jaws to a
        river,
and there's no one but the two of us to end its short, wet
        life.

My Wife's Brassieres

Strange flocked birds frighten,
clipped on the basement clothesline,
splayed open, hanging by shoulder straps,
nearly flat, curveless, lacking a bodied,
embracing circle. I duck
through them, a cold metal clasp
brushes my cheek. I turn on the lights;
they change, become no flock, but a menagerie.
A satiny blue butterfly, dark swirls
mimicking eyes. Further back,
skin-toned cups bulge
like the sightless tan lumps
of a cave lizard's eyes.
A dark one hangs like a bat
waiting night. One plain white,
rust stained, dries on its perch.
She's rinsed and washed the right cup
time and again,
this biopsy-born slaughtered dove.
She'll wash again tonight.

Toenails Diary

I cut my fingernails all the time, and every time I think to cut them, they need cutting. Now, for instance. And yet, I never, to the best of my knowledge, cut my toenails.
　　　　　—Rosencrantz, in Tom Stoppard's *Rosencrantz and Guildenstern Are Dead*

April 1: Melinda complains that, during the night, my toenails kept scratching her ankles, shows me red marks.

April 2: More marks. I say it must be the dog, sleeping at her feet, dreaming and snapping at what he mistakes for squirrels.

April 5: Same complaint as April 1. Little left toe snagged on stitching inside toe of sock. Ripped hole in gray silk Pierre Cardin. Darn.

April 9: Dog slept in Melinda's spot on bed. Melinda recovering at St. Elizabeth's from surgery to repair torn Achilles' tendon. Injured while sleeping. Tear was clean and easy to repair. Social Worker interviews me tomorrow.

April 10: Melinda coming home later. Social Worker asked about my anger (nonexistent), our cutlery (dull; we own no sharpener).

April 15: Bought new slippers, sole separated from old pair in front. Couldn't fit in usual 10s. Bought 11s. A little loose.

April 19: Toenails beginning to curl under selves. Hard to fit in shoes. Why no open toes on men's dress style Hush Puppies?

April 21: Must be walking funny, as I need to rest with sore feet elevated. Melinda does same with post-surgery foot.

April 25: Melinda walking better. Me, worse.

April 30: Spring. Sandal season.

Begging at a Statue,

you get used to being refused. Holding
your cup, your bowl, your shallow saucer
beneath the stone hands of a goddess,
a satyr, a nymph, or a king whose outstretched
arms both delineate and embrace his realm,
whose outstretched arms bear everything
and nothing, the fat king whose belly stretches
his tunic, the stone-carved tunic, to bursting,
holding your cup to him and receiving nothing
prepares you for a day of marketplace begging,
a day of asking for the smallest of coins
from women buying the day's fish or squid,
from servants buying their master's bread or bunches
of chard or bushels of figs and pomegranates
and being refused. So Diogenes began each day
begging from a statue. When I wake, shower,
shave, dress, drink coffee on my drive to work,
for what am I prepared? I should build a house
of statue, fill it with stone furniture, stone appliances,
stone food. The dining room table is set
with a plaster rack of lamb, the marble
refrigerator stocked full behind a never-opening door,
and a plasticine servant pours painted cabernet,
forever falling from bottle to glass. This device,
this constant-expressioned footman,
not even a fountain pouring water like one
Diogenes may have found, a poor indentured girl
dumping water from ewer into barrel
for no reason. Though she never forbade it,

he was too kind to take, with cupped hands,
a drink from her stream. He asked and asked
and asked yet she never changed expression.

An Alp

Ballantyne runs uphill, but not as steep
as the Alp rising where Ballantyne dead ends into Holland.
That mountain wasn't there when we bought the house
or when we did the final walkthrough and found
a dead skunk covered by a Hefty bag on our front lawn.
The skunk, we moved; the Alp, we can't,
so I bike to work around its base,
too out of shape to *Tour de France* my way
right up one side and down the other.
It blocks out winter sun, so nothing melts around our house
till mid-June, and kids from the Alp's south side
come to our street to make snowmen,
and their parents ask, "How'd a Swiss Alp get to Central
        New York?"
You dumbass, I think, *it could be French or German*,
and I'm like Mad King Ludwig, building a fairy tale castle
        here.
Except, like I said, we wouldn't have moved here
had we seen the Alp. Since taking up this residence,
and giving directions to everyone—friends,
furniture delivery men, the police who came when some
        climber
set up base camp in my dog's house—
and saying the world Alp—Alp, Alp, Alp, Alp—
We're down the street from the Alp,
I think the word sounds dumb, or maybe bad,
silently malicious, like something on your body,
lump, cyst, or polyp. I want to move
because this Alp rises like a symbol for my life,
corresponds to all the horse-sized polyps and cysts
I need to hack or lance my way through

on the road to success and riches.
It doesn't matter what those bumps stand for,
everyone's got them. Everyone's waiting
for that Century 21 sign down the street
to say SOLD, be taken down
by the moving-in family of happy, helpful Sherpas.

Last Words

Told performing again would kill her,
Anna Pavlova said, "Get my swan costume ready."
But how did she dance? Silent, putting on
her pointe shoes, silent when the music started,
silent still when the curtain fell and she fell,
those were her last words, defiant, not incoherent
like Henry VIII's "Monks, monks, monks!"
or pathetically lost like Louisa May Alcott's
"Is it not meningitis?" If you're dead,
does it matter? In *Little Women*, Beth March dies
but her sisters go on, her life meaningful
to the tune of Jo's poem, *blurred and blotted,*
faulty and feeble, hope and faith
born of sorrow. Those words aren't facts.
What about those who die absent facts?
What if Dylan Thomas was wrong and eighteen
wasn't a record? Or if he didn't say that?
At least he wasn't overly poetic—e.g., Walter
de la Mare's "Too late for fruit, too soon
for flowers." So move to Tahiti to die
where there's always Gaughin-y colored plants.
If someone records my last words,
I hope I say, "I'm in Tahiti,"
and I die with a dark-skinned woman
arranging red lily-like plants at my bedside,
my wife not far off (but far enough off
she doesn't hear any cry of pain, or, worse,
that terrible exhale of my last breath,
sound of me collapsing on myself). I hope
she's off with her feet in a clear, cold stream,
reading something, maybe *Little Women,*

thinking Jo triumphs by marrying the professor,
certain that is so, no matter what
feminist critics say or what is true. What will matter
when I'm gone? Oscar Wilde's last words—
"Either that wallpaper goes, or I do"—
are the saddest. That wallpaper's still there,
Jo March is still married, it wasn't meningitis,
but mercury poisoning. I'm sad
there was no swan costume, a long,
lithe neck curling heavenward while Anna danced,
up on her toes to get out of this life
quick and graceful as smoke disperses.

About the Author

Gary Leising is the author of two poetry chapbooks of poems, *Fastened to a Dying Animal* (Pudding House) and *Temple of Bones* (Finishing Line Press). His work has appeared in many literary journals, including recent and forthcoming poems in *Cincinnati Review, Gargoyle, Prairie Schooner,* and *River Styx.* He lives in upstate New York, with his wife and two sons, where he teaches creative writing and poetry at Utica College.

Our Mission

The mission of Brick Road Poetry Press is to publish and promote poetry that entertains, amuses, edifies, and surprises a wide audience of appreciative readers. We are not qualified to judge who deserves to be published, so we concentrate on publishing what we enjoy. Our preference is for poetry geared toward dramatizing the human experience in language rich with sensory image and metaphor, recognizing that poetry can be, at one and the same time, both familiar as the perspiration of daily labor and as outrageous as a carnival sideshow.

BrickRoad
Poetry Press
About the Prize

The Brick Road Poetry Prize, established in 2010, is awarded annually for the best book-length poetry manuscript. Entries are accepted August 1st through November 1st. The winner receives $1000 and publication. For details on our preferences and the complete submission guidelines, please visit our website at www.brickroadpoetrypress.com.